Cocaine

Cocaine

Elaine Landau

Franklin Watts
A Division of Scholastic Inc.
New York • Toronto • London • Auckland • Sydney
Mexico City • New Delhi • Hong Kong
Danbury, Connecticut

For Sara Sutin

Note to readers: Definitions for words in **bold** can be found in the Glossary at the back of this book.

Photographs © 2003: AP/Wide World Photos: 48 (Angela Gaul), 46 (Mark Stehle); Bridgeman Art Library International Ltd., London/New York/Barbara Singer: 10; Corbis Images: 28 (ER Productions), 5, 30 (Image 100), 8 (Charles & Josette Lenars), 16 (Chuck Savage), 11, 13; Fundamental Photos, New York/Richard Megna: cover; Photo Researchers, NY: 6 (Dr. Morley Read), 15 (Tek Image), 26 (Jim Varney); PhotoEdit: 5, 22, 41 (Billy E. Barnes), 37 (David Kelly Crow), 44 (Spencer Grant), 38 (Jeff Greenberg), 40 (Dennis MacDonald), 50 (John Neubauer), 20 (Michael Newman), 18 (Jonathan Nourok), 32 (Mark Richards), 34 (David Young-Wolff); Stock Boston: 24 (Bob Daemmrich), 2 (Peter Menzel), 29 (Frank Siteman); Visuals Unlimited/Frank T. Awbrey: 27.

The photograph on the cover shows cocaine. The photograph opposite the title page shows people picking the leaves off the coca plant.

Library of Congress Cataloging-in-Publication Data

Landau, Elaine
    Cocaine / by Elaine Landau
        p. cm. — (Watts library)
    Summary: Discusses the health issues and dangers associated with cocaine and crack, the history of its use in the United States, and treatment options for those with an addiction to these drugs.
    ISBN 0-531-12026-0 (lib. bdg.)   0-531-16667-8 (pbk.)
    1. Cocaine habit—Juvenile literature. 2. Cocaine—Juvenile literature. [1. Cocaine. 2. Crack (Drug). 3. Drug Abuse.] I. Title. II. Series.
HV5810 .L36 2003
613.8′4—dc21
                                                2002008884

Contents

Cocaine comes from the leaves of the coca plant.

Chapter One

History of Cocaine

Cocaine is hardly a new drug. More than two thousand years ago, native peoples in South America were aware of the potent powers of the coca plant. The plant is simply an evergreen shrub with reddish bark and yellowish-green flowers. Yet this ordinary looking plant has remained in demand through the ages. It is the source of cocaine.

Long before European explorers came to the Americas, coca was often part of the native peoples' healing practices and rituals. They chewed on the leaves and also made them into a tea. Sometimes, they applied the leaves to wounds as a healing balm.

The coca plant grew wild in Peru where the Incas had established a highly advanced civilization. At first, the use of coca had been somewhat restricted. For the most part, it was reserved for the Inca emperor, his family, and high officials. They enjoyed the pleasurable feeling it provided. The emperor would distribute it to his subjects when they

The coca plant grew wild in the lands of the Incas.

performed a particularly valuable service for him. The Incas found it helpful in relieving hunger pangs and exhaustion.

Europeans and the Coca Plant

By the time Spanish explorers arrived in South America, coca was more widely used by the Incas and other native peoples. The Spanish **conquistadores** brought the plant back to Europe. But unlike other gifts from the Americas, such as coffee and tobacco, it did not become immediately popular. This was largely because the leaves from coca plant lost their **potency** during the long sea voyage from Peru.

By the middle of the 1800s, European interest in coca began to grow. Some of the interest had been generated by an Italian doctor named Paolo Mantegazza. When Mantegazza visited Lima, Peru, he noticed a widespread local custom there. People ingested a mixture containing coca leaves. The native people also sucked on wads of these leaves. At times they kept the leaves against their cheeks for several hours. The leaves seemed to give the native people lots of energy as well as to boost their spirits. In 1859 Mantegazza published a paper on the effects of coca, and other Europeans became curious about the plant.

Nevertheless, the cocaine craze that would later sweep Europe might have never occurred if not for the work of Albert Nieman. In 1860 Nieman, a German **pharmacology** graduate student, successfully isolated cocaine from the coca leaf. For this work, he earned his doctoral degree, but his

VIN MARIANI

POPULAR
FRENCH TONIC WINE

*Fortifies and Refreshes Body & Brain
Restores Health and Vitality*

This is an early advertisement for Angelo Mariani's cocaine-laced beverage.

accomplishment had unexpected and far-reaching consequences. Previously, the only source of the drug we know as cocaine was coca leaves, and these tended to lose their vigor with shipping and storage. Now things changed. Cocaine now became available as a separate substance. Before long, the word came into common usage. The word "cocaine" first appeared in a British pharmaceutical journal in 1874. Soon afterward the drug found its way into a variety of wines, medicines, and home remedies.

A shrewd French businessman named Angelo Mariani was among the first to profitably market cocaine. In 1863, he concocted a new wine drink called Mariani's Coca Wine or Dr. Mariani's French Tonic. This beverage contained 6 milligrams of cocaine per ounce. Touted as a potent wine tonic, it became the latest sensation in Paris cafes.

Mariani launched a massive publicity campaign for the drink. He actively sought celebrity endorsements, which he featured in printed advertisements for his wine. Mariani's satisfied customers included the inventor Thomas Edison, author Robert Louis Stevenson, President William McKinley, and actress Sarah Bernhardt. Mariani won praises for his wine from Pope Leo XIII, sixteen heads of state, and eighteen thousand physicians.

Shortly thereafter, in 1884, doctors began to explore cocaine's possible medical uses. Some doctors used it as a **local anesthetic**—a substance that numbs the body in a specific area—for ear, eye, and throat surgeries.

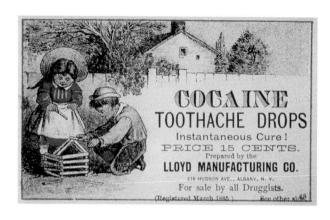

Cocaine became an important ingredient in many health aids and medicines.

Drug companies geared up to meet the growing medical demand for cocaine. Some even sent groups of workers to Ecuador, Peru, and Colombia to increase their coca supply. Hoping to enhance profits, drug companies soon expanded cocaine's possible uses. They added it to thousands of medicines, which people took for headaches, toothaches, and a variety of other aches and pains. Cocaine was viewed as a sort of wonder drug that could cure anything. One pharmaceutical company described the drug's effects: "[It] could make the coward brave, the silent eloquent, ... the sufferer insensitive to pain."

Cocaine in the United States

By the end of the 1800s cocaine was taken in many forms and was a common ingredient in numerous medications on both sides of the Atlantic. In 1896, the *New York Herald* newspaper ran the story, "Whole Town Mad for Cocaine." Indeed, sometimes it seemed to be. At that point in U.S. history, cocaine was a completely legal and readily available substance. Since it was reasonably priced, its popularity continued to skyrocket.

Cocaine was commonly used to treat various skin conditions. It was also prescribed for shingles, a painful disease that affects the sensory nerves. Many people felt that there was nothing better for asthma, a respiratory disease. One Connecticut pharmacist complained that desperate asthma sufferers who ran out of their favorite remedy often came to his house for it at all hours of the night.

Large numbers of people who took this supposed feel-good drug were unaware of the consequences. However, before long, these became all too apparent. There were reports of cocaine-related heart attacks and strokes. People suffered various mental disturbances as well. Some became paranoid, claiming that close friends or family members were trying to kill them. Others seemed unhinged. One man jumped from a window believing that he could fly.

The powerful **addictive** quality of cocaine also came to light. In 1902 Annie Meyers, a Chicago woman described as "a proper Christian," wrote about her nightmarish experiences with cocaine. This shocking exposé revealed the truth about the drug. For the first time, the public was exposed to the negative consequences of an extremely popular substance. People began to look at cocaine differently. Similar newspaper and magazine stories that followed reinforced this new point of view. They all linked cocaine to moral downfall and physical ailments.

Dope in Coke?

In 1886 the popular soft drink Coca-Cola was made with a cocaine-laced syrup. Cocaine did not remain an ingredient for long. By 1903, cocaine was removed from the beverage.

The Tide Turns

Before long, the tide of public opinion turned against cocaine. In 1910 President William Taft publicly described cocaine as a dangerous and highly addictive drug. In his annual message to Congress, the president noted: "Cocaine is more appalling in its effects than any other habit-forming drug used in the United States."

A movement for reform was soon set in motion. Many states had already passed some type of legislation to try to control widespread cocaine use. Finally, the U.S. Congress passed the Harrison Narcotics Act of 1914. This federal law banned the use of cocaine without a physician's prescription.

Law enforcement officers made a special effort to stop cocaine traffic and the drug's use steadily declined. New drugs known as amphetamines gained popularity and began to replace cocaine in America's drug culture. As an illegal drug, cocaine had become difficult to get, while amphetamines were inexpensive and widely available. By World War II (1939–1945), it seemed as if cocaine use was out of fashion.

William Howard Taft was the first president to recognize the harmful effects of cocaine.

Back in Style

Nevertheless, years later cocaine would become a widely sought after drug again. Despite disastrous early experiences with it, substantial numbers of people rediscovered cocaine as a recreational drug in the 1960s and 1970s. As the term "recreational" implies, people take such drugs for fun, not for any possible medicinal value. Many of the people who now used this high-priced drug were music, sports, or show business celebrities. Cocaine became increasingly popular among the wealthy and glamorous.

It was obvious to hospital emergency room staffs across the country that cocaine use was on the rise. Cocaine-related deaths and medical problems were becoming increasingly common. The situation worsened in the mid-1980s when **crack** cocaine appeared on the drug scene. Crack is a potent, highly addictive form of cocaine that can be smoked. It was sold in vials in small amounts and was therefore less expensive. Crack's low price made it affordable to a far broader cross section of the population.

When crack appeared on the scene, cocaine use in the United States peaked for a second time. Large numbers of people were using the drug, and the problem reached **epidemic** proportions. Many of the users were young. In a 1986 nationally televised address, President Ronald Reagan said that cocaine was "killing a whole generation of our children" and "tearing our country apart." The public became highly alarmed over the situation, just as it had nearly a century before. The available statistics supported the level of concern. Between 1979 and 1985, the number of people coming to hospital emergency rooms with cocaine-related problems jumped

An Equally Unhealthy Alternative

Amphetamines heighten physical and mental activity. They are sometimes called "speed" or "wake-ups" because they prevent sleep.

14

from 1,931 to 9,403. Three years later, in 1988, the number skyrocketed to 46,020.

In time, stricter drug-law enforcement, along with enhanced drug education programs and treatment options, calmed things down a bit. Government-sponsored studies showed that cocaine use decreased among twelfth graders from 6.2 percent in 1999 to 5.0 percent in 2000. Crack use declined from 2.7 percent to 2.2 percent among students in the same grade as well.

Crack cocaine has a rocklike consistency.

This trend also seemed true for society as a whole. As the negative consequences of this dangerous drug became better known, cocaine deaths in 2000 either decreased or remained stable in many cities, including Detroit, Honolulu, Miami, Philadelphia, San Diego, and San Francisco.

As a result, you don't hear as much about cocaine today. Occasionally, a celebrity is in the news for possessing the drug or dying as a result of it. Some former cocaine users also began using other drugs, such as heroin. Yet is the cocaine problem really over? National Institute on Drug Abuse (NIDA) researchers report that early in the new millennium cocaine-related deaths increased substantially in Phoenix and Seattle, as well as in several other areas. Some think these numbers could continue to climb. You might not hear as much about cocaine anymore, but unfortunately, the drug has not gone away.

Cocaine can take over people's lives, leading them to do things, such as stealing, just to get more drugs.

Chapter Two

A Closer Look at Cocaine

My parents threw me out when I was on cocaine. They said they couldn't trust me. I knew they were right. I'd lie about going to school. Lie about stealing money from them. I'd lie about everything—just to get my drugs. My Aunt Lynn took me in. She'd always been my favorite aunt. She stood up for me, but I let her down. I stole from her too. I was ashamed but I couldn't help it. That's what happens when you use cocaine.

Jeff, a former cocaine user

When people buy cocaine on the street, they may get more than they bargained for. Drug dealers sometimes mix in other substances.

It may seem unlikely that a fine white powder could cause the reaction Jeff described. Yet these feelings have been voiced countless times by cocaine users. Undeniably, this drug warrants a closer look.

When people buy cocaine on the street, they are usually not purchasing pure cocaine. The drug is mixed with other substances. Drug dealers add these to cocaine to stretch their supply and maximize profits. Added ingredients may include white powdery look-alikes, such as cornstarch, talcum powder, or sugar. However, in some cases, cocaine may be mixed with more harmful substances, resulting in serious injury to the user or even death.

Taking Cocaine

People take cocaine in several ways. Some snort or inhale it. The drug enters the body through the lining of their nose. Snorting is usually done in one of two ways. Sometimes the person uses a tiny spoon to scoop up a small quantity of cocaine. He or she brings the spoon up to one nostril while

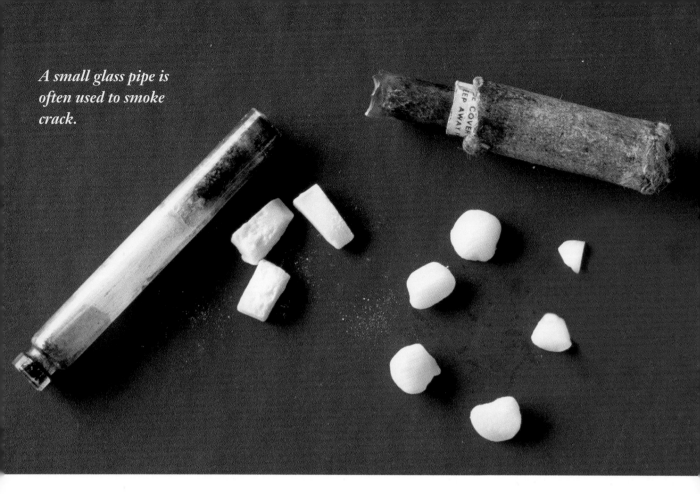

A small glass pipe is often used to smoke crack.

holding the other nostril closed. The individual breathes in quickly, drawing the cocaine up the nasal passage.

In the second way cocaine is snorted, the drug is laid out on a smooth surface, such as a mirror or a piece of glass. Using a razor blade, the person separates the cocaine into thin lines. The user then inhales these powdery lines through a thin straw or tightly rolled dollar bill.

Other cocaine users inject the drug directly into their bloodstream with a hypodermic syringe and needle. They are injecting the same drug that others snort. However, first they dissolve the powder in water or another fluid.

French Fries

In some places, crack is sold in three-inch sticks with ridges. These are called french fries.

Smoking Crack

Crack is cocaine in a form that can be smoked. To prepare crack, cocaine hydrochloride—cocaine in powder form—is processed with baking soda and water. It is heated to remove the hydrochloride. The process is known as **freebasing** because the cocaine base is freed from cocaine hydrocholoride. The end result is a smokable form of cocaine. When cocaine is smoked, large amounts of the drug rapidly enter the user's system. Crack looks like small lumps, or rocks. That's why crack is sometimes called rock cocaine.

Because smoking cocaine causes a much faster rise in drug levels in the body, users claim that a crack **high** is more exhilarating than what they experience when snorting or injecting cocaine. The faster the drug is absorbed, the more intense the high. When cocaine is snorted, it takes 3 to 4 minutes for the drug to reach the brain. Cocaine reaches the brain in 15 seconds when injected in liquid form. But if smoked, it takes just 6 to 8 seconds for the drug to get to the brain. A cocaine user compared snorting cocaine to smoking crack as follows:

> *I would say that snorting is more controllable and basing [smoking crack] seems to be an obsession. Once you start, you don't want to stop. . . . Snorting, you can take a hit and not think about it until like a day or so or maybe even a month. But with base, it's there and when it's gone. . . . I've never felt so angry about something being gone. That's crazy, it really is. It's sick.*

People often get trapped in a deadly cycle with crack. After the initial high wears off, the user craves more of the drug to fight off the feelings of withdrawal.

With the introduction of crack, many more people became cocaine users. Before crack, cocaine was only available in powder form, which was extremely expensive. In some areas, a gram of cocaine could cost as much as four hundred dollars. Regular users might spend hundreds or even thousands of dollars a week on it. But a small vial of crack could be bought for from ten to fifteen dollars. This lower price made the drug affordable to many more people—including young people.

Some people said that crack's appeal was irresistible. For a small amount of money, they claimed to experience supreme pleasure. After using the drug, people would experience a tremendous letdown. To escape the lows, crack users sought still another high in the form of more crack. Often they became caught up in a vicious downward spiral. Many swore that it was no longer a matter of using a recreational drug at will. Crack now dominated their lives, and some felt there was no escape. As one young crack user described the feeling:

Crack is more than a drug. It becomes a way of life. I used to have all kinds of dreams. I dreamed of graduating from high school and of getting married. I used to think that maybe I could even break into show business. But crack ended all my dreams. You cook it, smoke it, and think about how you can get more. There isn't room in your brain for anything else. When you're on crack, nothing matters except staying high.

What's in a Name?

The drug crack got its name from the crackling sound heard when it is heated.

It only takes a short while for cocaine to affect the body after it has been inhaled.

Chapter Three

Physical Effects

When a person takes cocaine, he or she will feel its effects almost immediately. Cocaine stimulates an area in the brain that regulates pleasurable sensations. The user often feels exhilarated and full of vigor. He or she may also seem mentally alert, and the need for food and sleep may decrease.

Some people claim that the drug allows them to work or study more effectively. Others say just the opposite is true. They feel too rushed, anxious, and disorganized

When the drug wears off, people often feel tense and strange.

to accomplish very much. One college student recalled the feeling this way, "[I] just couldn't study at all while I was doing it [cocaine]. . . . I couldn't focus on anything."

In any case, a cocaine high is a brief experience. If snorted, cocaine's effects usually last from fifteen to thirty minutes. When smoked, the drug's high is gone after five to ten minutes. Many cocaine users have described themselves as feeling tense or edgy at that point.

Drug Effects

The effects of any drug will vary with the amount of the drug taken, the person's prior drug experience and emotional stability, and whether the drug is taken with other drugs or alcohol.

Effects on the Body

People who use cocaine may think they know how they feel at the moment. However, often they are not aware of what the drug is really doing to their bodies. Cocaine's immediate physical effects include a rise in blood pressure and body temperature along with increased heart and breathing rates. The person's pupils become **dilated**, or larger, and there's a narrowing of blood vessels throughout the body. Cocaine can also affect the body in many other ways.

Cocaine can create a disturbance in the brain's electrical signals. This may result in brain seizures. In some instances, the electrical signals regulating the muscles that control breathing are disrupted. When this happens, respiratory failure occurs, and the person stops breathing. At times, cocaine

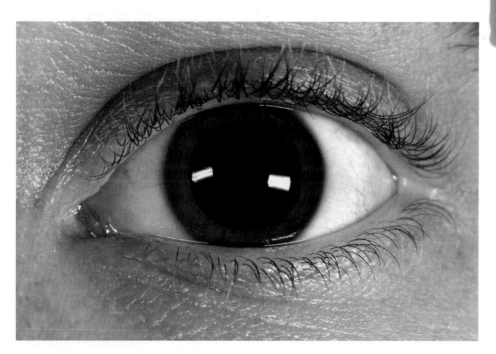

A dilated pupil is one of the signs that someone is using cocaine.

27

users also suffer strokes. The rise in blood pressure caused by the drug ruptures blood vessels in the brain.

Since cocaine constricts or narrows the heart's blood vessels, the heart has to work harder and faster to move blood through the body. Have you ever tried to squeeze into a tight pair of pants? It isn't easy. Similarly, it is difficult for the heart to pump blood through narrowed vessels. In some cases, the constriction of the blood vessels has resulted in severe chest pains or even a heart attack.

Cocaine can also interfere with the heart's pumping action. This can cause disturbances in the heart's rhythm—the heart may beat irregularly or stop altogether. Cocaine has caused heart attacks in young people with no history of heart trouble.

Cocaine has been known to affect the human heart, causing fatal heart attacks in some cases.

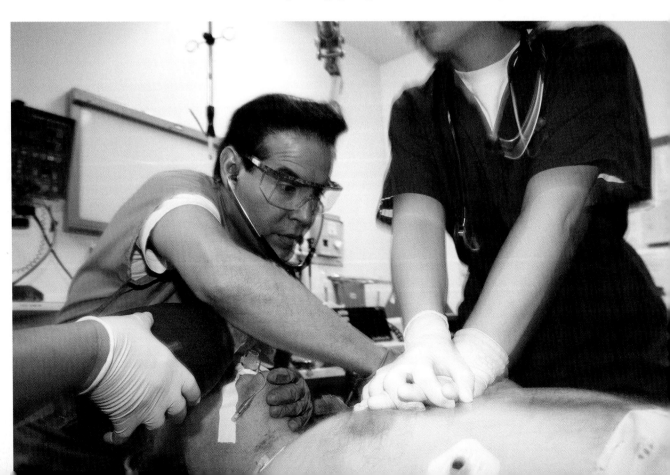

Some of these individuals have been first-time users of the drug. For them, their first experimentation with cocaine was their last.

Cocaine can bring out the worst in people, causing them to become violent.

Cocaine and Mental Health

Despite what some people might think, cocaine is not a feel-good drug. It causes violent or erratic behavior in some people. In one case, a girl slapped her little sister so hard that the child's nose bled. The young girl had borrowed a CD without asking permission. A teenage boy who used cocaine lost his job at a fast-food restaurant. While taking the drug, he was not able to get to work on time or do what was expected of him. The worst psychological effects frequently occur in those who use substantial amounts of the drug on a daily basis. This is known as **cocaine bingeing**.

29

During these periods, users sometimes describe themselves as being coked out. Often they become irritable, anxious, and restless. They may also feel confused and be quick to lash out if confronted.

A condition known as cocaine psychosis is particularly common among crack users. Those affected by this ailment are severely delusional and believe that someone or something

is trying to harm them. Often they also think they possess godlike powers. They may believe that they could survive on another planet or that they are going to live forever. Sometimes these individuals are plagued by **hallucinations**—seeing or hearing things that are not there—and lose touch with reality. People using large amounts of cocaine frequently experience a hallucination known as coke bugs. These users think they see and feel insects crawling across their bodies. One such woman said she would pick the bugs off her arms and legs and put them in a glass of water beside her bed. When she awoke the following morning, she would find the glass filled with pieces of her own skin.

Cocaine and Pregnancy

Pregnant women who use cocaine risk harming their unborn babies as well as themselves. Using cocaine during the early months of pregnancy can result in miscarriage or stillbirth. In such situations, a woman could lose both her baby and her freedom. That's what happened to Regina McKnight, a twenty-four-year-old North Carolina woman, who in 1999 delivered a stillborn infant after having used crack during her pregnancy. She was charged with "homicide by child abuse" and tried for the offense. After deliberating for just fifteen minutes, the jury convicted McKnight. She was sentenced to twelve years in prison.

Following the verdict, Greg Hembree, the prosecutor in the case, said, "If the child had been smothered by its mother

This mother used crack while she was pregnant. Children of crack users often have learning difficulties.

two weeks after being born, there'd be no question about prosecution. The only difference here is, this was two weeks before the child would have been born. It is still part of a parent's fundamental responsibility to protect children." Pointing out that at the time she went to trial Regina McKnight was again pregnant, Hembree added, "I know for sure that her baby isn't going to die from crack cocaine this time. That's one thing I know."

Children who survive exposure to cocaine as a fetus can experience problems after they are born. They are more likely to be delivered prematurely and have **low birth weights**— weigh less than they should at birth. Such babies are also more likely to be victims of **sudden infant death syndrome**, or crib death. In these cases, seemingly healthy babies die in their sleep for no apparent reason.

During the late 1980s and early 1990s babies born to mothers using cocaine were often labeled crack babies. At the time, these children's futures were thought to be especially grim. They were believed to suffer from severe, irreversible damage, which included lowered levels of intelligence as well as problems developing social skills.

Fortunately, research has since shown that the situation is not that bleak. With proper treatment the majority of crack-exposed babies recover and seem perfectly normal. Nevertheless, this does not mean that they are unaffected by their mother's crack use.

Scientists are now finding that **prenatal**, or before birth, exposure to cocaine can lead to subtle problems later. Often these difficulties arise in areas that are crucial to school success. Many such children have a harder time blocking out distractions. They may also find it difficult to concentrate for long periods.

Double Trouble

Pregnant women should avoid both cocaine and alcohol. Mixing the two, however, can have deadly consequences for anyone. The liver combines these drugs to form a third substance called **cocaethylene**. While cocaethylene intensifies the cocaine high, it also increases the risk of sudden death.

For *addicts*, the drug becomes their lives. They no longer want to do the things they used to do, such as play sports.

Chapter Four

Addiction and Treatment

I'm sorry I ever touched cocaine. I was expelled from school. My friends left me. My mother cries all the time and my father won't even speak to me anymore. I lost all this and I still want that stupid drug. I feel bad most of the time. No one should have to feel like this. No one should go near cocaine.

Angeles, a recovering cocaine addict

Cocaine is an extremely addictive drug. Countless cocaine users claim that their desire for it soon became overwhelming. Someone may begin using cocaine to feel good, but before long, this can backfire. As that person takes more of the drug, he or she develops a tolerance for it. The same amount of cocaine will no longer make that person feel as good as it once did. Higher cocaine doses and increasingly frequent use of the drug become necessary. Many cocaine users say that in time they needed significant amounts of the drug just to feel normal.

Cocaine can ruin lives. In some cases, the drug causes people to lose sight of what is really important. It is not uncommon for cocaine users to rely on the drug they desperately seek to provide unrealistic benefits. John, a former cocaine addict, described what cocaine meant to him this way:

I put all my faith and hope into cocaine. While on cocaine, I felt all powerful. Cocaine made me feel as if I could solve all the world's problems with nothing more than a thought. The reality was I was part of the problem. Cocaine never lived up to its promise.

All forms of cocaine are addictive. However, crack has been known to hook users especially quickly. This may be due to the drug's rapidly produced highs followed by the profound lows, which leave users desperate for more. When people become crack or cocaine addicts, the drug rules. They soon start to lose interest in work, school, family, friends, and sports. Many are prepared to lie, cheat, or steal to get the drug.

To an addict, only the drug matters.

Stars and Celebrities

Fame and fortune cannot ward off the ravages of cocaine addiction. Such celebrities as professional baseball player Darryl Strawberry and actor Robert Downey, Jr., have lost valuable career and personal opportunities, as well as done jail time, due to their drug addiction problems. Numerous other celebrities, including musicians and artists, have had to deal with cocaine addiction as well.

Treatment Options

Treatment of cocaine addiction tends to be complex. Besides the physical addiction to the drug, there are often social, family, and environmental factors involved. For cocaine addicts, the road to recovery is frequently long and difficult. Unfortunately, there is no shortage of people who need help with this problem. Drug treatment centers in many parts of the country largely report that cocaine is the drug most often abused by their clients. At times, people of varying ages need help. When young people are involved, the therapies used with adults are modified to meet the needs of youths.

There are drug treatment centers all across the country designed to help people fight their addictions to drugs like cocaine.

Yet before any treatment can begin, the person's body must be purged or cleansed of the drug. This process is known as **detoxification**, often called detox for short. Once drug free, recovering users must find ways to handle their need, or craving, for cocaine.

There is still no specific drug regularly used to treat cocaine addiction. However, the National Institute on Drug Abuse (NIDA) is actively working on identifying and testing numerous medications for future use. The goal is to find a drug to block or greatly reduce the effects of cocaine. Researchers are also looking at medications that will reduce the craving cocaine addicts must deal with. More than sixty drugs are presently being studied as possible treatments for cocaine addiction. In the meantime, antidepressant drugs are frequently prescribed for recovering addicts experiencing mood swings while trying to stay drug free.

Behavioral Therapy

For many people, therapy to change behaviors that led to their drug involvement is extremely helpful. **Contingency management** is one type of **behavioral therapy**. With this method patients are rewarded for staying off cocaine. Those who remain drug free are given points that can be exchanged for desirable items such as a gym membership or movie tickets. The rewards chosen for the program are always healthy alternatives to cocaine use.

Acupuncture for Addicts?

At a number of drug treatment centers, **acupuncture** has been used with some success to lessen cocaine cravings.

Talking with a therapist is a good way to help fight an addiction.

In a very special contingency management program at Johns Hopkins University, researchers have woven important workplace skills into the reward program. There, recovering addicts earn vouchers for food and rent by working as data-entry operators. Their wages increase as their skills improve. However, they lose earnings if urine testing reveals any evidence of drug use. Researchers attribute the program's success to the financial benefits offered. They feel it helps provide a potent reason to resist the temptation of cocaine.

Cognitive behavioral therapy is another approach used in cocaine addiction treatment. This form of therapy teaches patients skills to better cope with their drug problem. Ideally, they learn to handle or avoid situations in which they would be tempted to use cocaine. They also learn to face problems that might have led them to escape through drugs.

As National Institute on Drug Abuse director Dr. Alan I. Leshner noted, "Addiction affects every aspect of an individual's interaction with the world. People in recovery need to know how to control their behavior, how to function in their families [and] how to go back to work."

A Difficult Road to Recovery

Patients with extremely severe cocaine-related problems may be treated in a **residential drug treatment center**. Some treatment facilities are especially geared to helping young users. Often patients live at the treatment center for six months

Receiving job training while at a treatment center helps people to build a new life, free of drugs.

Is Your Friend Using Cocaine?

Sometimes it is hard to tell if a friend is using cocaine. However, the Center for Substance Abuse Prevention notes that the following symptoms are often warning signs:
- Red, bloodshot eyes
- A runny nose or frequent sniffing
- A change in groups of friends
- Acting withdrawn, depressed, tired, or careless about personal appearance
- A loss of interest in school, family, or activities he or she used to enjoy
- Frequent need for money

You may be able to help. The center recommends that you encourage your friend to get professional assistance.

to a year. At these facilities, they may be offered a broad range of services, including both individual and family therapy as well as job training.

In less serious cases, recovering users live at home while attending therapy sessions several times a week. Many recovering cocaine users also find strength and support through self-help groups such as Cocaine Anonymous or Narcotics Anonymous. In these organizations recovering cocaine users attend meetings where they share their experiences and help one another remain drug free.

Leaving cocaine behind can be a challenge. Many former users claim that they still experience cravings for cocaine long after giving the drug up. Yet the rewards of doing so are well worth it. One former cocaine user described his feelings about it as follows:

Even though I have rebuilt my life, my career, family, etc.,
I realize it is still going to be a lifelong fight to continue to be
able to resist the draw this addictive substance has. What stops
me from using again is the fear I have of going back into a
jail cell, and losing what I have worked so hard to regain . . . .
Now . . . after each time I resist, I feel better about myself,
and more resolute not to ever again use.

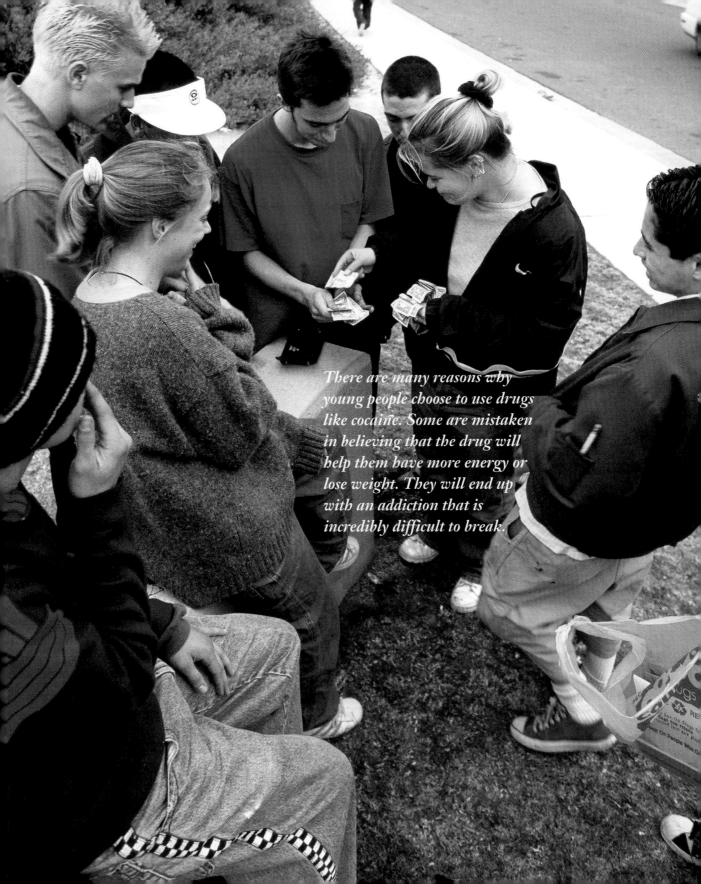

There are many reasons why young people choose to use drugs like cocaine. Some are mistaken in believing that the drug will help them have more energy or lose weight. They will end up with an addiction that is incredibly difficult to break.

Chapter Five

Costs of Cocaine Use

One young woman named Rebecca turned to cocaine because she believed it would make her thin. She wanted to look like a model, but ended up becoming a drug addict. "I got thin but the good stuff never happened. I always had a runny nose and my hair started falling out. . . . After a while I wasn't using the drug to get thin anymore. I was using it because I couldn't stop. I was out of control."

In the end, Rebecca was among the lucky ones. She overcame her addiction and went on to enjoy a productive drug-free life. But for many people addicted to cocaine and other drugs, there is no happy ending.

A Costly Problem

In an effort to stop drug dealers, police departments have stepped up their patrols in areas known for selling drugs.

The cost of drug abuse is high both to the individual and society as a whole. Roughly half of all serious crimes are committed by people under the influence of cocaine or other drugs. Whole neighborhoods have been terrorized by rival drug gangs fighting over turf. Many gangs sell drugs to young

people. Unfortunately, at times young crack users become crack dealers to support their habit.

Americans spend $20 billion annually to wage a war on drugs. For the most part, the problem has been dealt with as a matter for the criminal justice system. A good deal of time and resources have been focused on eliminating international drug smuggling.

Bringing in the Goods

Bolivia, Colombia, and Peru produce 75 percent of the world's cocaine supply. Well-organized drug rings regularly send large cocaine shipments to Mexico, where they are broken down into smaller units to be smuggled into the United States. At times, land vehicles are used to bring cocaine across the Mexican border to points in the southwestern United States.

There are also drug smuggling routes through the Caribbean and the Bahamas to south Florida's shipping ports. Cocaine from South America is first airdropped to an island in the Bahamas or a specified point in the water just off the coast

Customs officials seize a bag filled with cocaine.

Tricks of the Drug Trade

In recent years, some drug traffickers have found a way to slip cocaine past customs inspectors and drug-sniffing dogs. They add charcoal, along with certain chemicals, to the cocaine, which turns it into a black odorless substance. In this form, it does not react if subjected to the usual chemical tests for cocaine. In some instances, the cocaine may even be molded into the shape of a common household object. Once the drug is in the United States, another chemical process is used to restore it to its original form. Then it is sold to drug dealers, who in turn sell it to their customers.

of Puerto Rico. From there, the cocaine is put on a fast-moving speedboat, from which it is transferred to a large coastal freighter. Well hidden within the freighter's cargo, the cocaine illegally enters the United States.

It has been argued that cocaine trafficking thrives because of the market for the drug in the United States and because of corruption on the part of some law enforcement officials in all the countries involved. Nevertheless, many local police officers, Federal Bureau of Investigation (FBI) agents, and Drug Enforcement Agency (DEA) agents have put their lives on the line to stop drug traffic. Every year authorities confiscate from hundreds to thousands of pounds of cocaine. Headlines like "Five Hundred Pounds of Cocaine Seized" or "Thirty Members of Drug Ring Captured" are not uncommon.

Stopping the Crime

Numerous law enforcement measures have also been taken to halt drug abuse within the United States. Stiffened penalties have meant incarceration for hundreds of thousands of drug users and sellers. Federal laws have also been passed allowing the homes and cars of drug dealers to be seized if used in the sale of drugs.

While stopping drug-related crimes is an essential part of solving the drug problem, there is more work to be done in the area of addictions to illegal drugs. Use of cocaine and other illegal and dangerous drugs remains a very real problem

Jail Time

In 2001 more than 500,000 people in the United States were in prison on drug-related charges. Approximately, 15 percent of these individuals were less than twenty-five years old.

Being caught with cocaine may lead to prison time. However, some judges are offering offenders a chance at rehabilitation.

today. Imprisoning addicts has not done much to help matters. Unfortunately, jailed addicts do not generally receive the treatment needed to remain drug free when released. Nearly 85 percent of those imprisoned for drug abuse use cocaine or other drugs after leaving prison. Frequently users are looked down on for being unable to stay off drugs, but as drug reformer Ethan Nadelman noted, "In every other realm of health care we blame the treatment provider if something goes wrong. Here we still blame the patient."

Exploring New Possibilities

Recently, people have begun to look for other answers. Tactics that combine legal and medical measures have been explored. The result has been the development of an increased number of drug courts that offer treatment options with prison penalties for violations. There is also a strengthened effort underway to extend insurance benefits to more fully cover drug abuse treatment and related mental health concerns.

Some people feel that an arsenal of innovative weapons must be on hand to fight cocaine use. Effective antidrug campaigns may need to include reforming the legal system so that it is more favorably disposed to treatment, new medications, and enhanced counseling programs. The world cannot afford to turn its backs on the problem. The financial and human costs of cocaine use are far too high.

Significant Savings

Treatment rather than prison time may also be a better choice financially. For example, in 2001, the cost of keeping someone in a New York State prison for a year was about $32,000. But a year in a New York residential drug treatment center only costs from $17,000 to $21,000. Outpatient care for drug addiction is even less at $2,700 to $4,500 per person, per year.

Timeline

1500s	Spanish conquistadores bring coca leaves from South America to Europe.
1859	Paolo Mantegazza, an Italian physician, publishes a paper on the effects of coca leaves.
1860	Albert Nieman, a German pharmacology student, isolates cocaine from the coca plant.
1863	Mariani's Coca Wine or Dr. Mariani's French Tonic, a drink containing significant amounts of cocaine, become popular in Paris.
1884	Doctors begin to use cocaine as a local anesthetic in ear, eye, and throat surgeries.
1886	Coca-Cola, a popular American beverage, is made with a cocaine-laced syrup.
1902	Annie Meyers writes a shocking exposé about her experiences with cocaine, revealing its highly addictive quality.
1903	Cocaine is removed from Coca-Cola.
1910	President William Taft denounces cocaine in his annual message to Congress.
1914	The Harrison Narcotics Act is passed, making cocaine illegal in the United States without a doctor's prescription.
1960s–1970s	Substantial number of people rediscover cocaine as a recreational drug.
mid-1980s	Crack appears on the drug scene, and its use is soon described as epidemic.
mid-1990s	Cocaine use decreases.
2000	Cocaine use is down throughout most of the United States.
2001	More than 500,000 people in the United States are in prison on drug-related charges.

Glossary

acupuncture—a medical procedure from China in which needles are placed beneath the patient's skin to relieve discomfort

behavioral therapy—therapy to change behaviors that lead to drug involvement and other problems

addictive—something that causes the body to become dependent on it

cocaethylene—a substance formed by the liver when cocaine and alcohol are used together

cocaine bingeing—using substantial amounts of cocaine on a daily basis

cognitive behavioral therapy—a type of behavioral therapy through which the patient learns better coping skills in dealing with drug-related problems

conquistador—a Spanish explorer and conqueror

contingency management—a type of behavioral therapy through which patients earn rewards for staying drug free

crack—an inexpensive form of cocaine that can be smoked

detoxification—the process of cleansing or purging the body of drugs

dilated—enlarged or widened

epidemic—a disease that is temporarily prevalent throughout a large area

freebasing—the process by which cocaine is chemically altered to remove other substances

hallucination—something seen or heard that is not there

high—a slang term used to describe the feeling of exhilaration derived from a drug

local anesthetic—a drug that deadens pain in a specific part of the body

low birth weight—weighing less than is desirable at birth

pharmacology—the science dealing with the preparation and effects of drugs

potency—strength or vigor

prenatal—prior to birth

residential drug treatment center—a facility where patients live while being treated for a drug problem

sudden infant death syndrome (SIDS)—a syndrome in which an infant dies while asleep for no apparent reason. SIDS has been identified as the major cause of infant death after the first month of life.

To Find Out More

Books

Bayer, Linda N. *Crack & Cocaine*. Philadelphia: Chelsea House Publications, 2000.

Gottfried, Ted. *Should Drugs Be Legalized?* Brookfield, CT: Twenty-First Century Books, 2000.

Holmes, Ann. *Effects of Cocaine and Crack Addiction*. Philadelphia: Chelsea House Publications, 1999.

Hyde, Margaret O. *Know About Drugs*. New York: Walker, 1996.

Oliver, Marilyn Tower. *Drugs: Should They Be Legalized?* Berkeley Heights, NJ: Enslow Publishers, 1999.

Robbins, Paul R. *Crack and Cocaine: Drug Dangers*. Berkeley Heights, NJ: Enslow Publishers, 1999.

McLaughlin, Miriam Smith. *Addiction: The High That Brings You Down*. Berkeley Heights, NJ: Enslow Publishers, 1997.

Swishers, Karen L., ed. *Legalizing Drugs*. San Diego, CA: Greenhaven Press, 1996.

Washburne, Caroline Kott. *Drug Abuse*. San Diego, CA: Lucent Books, 1996.

Wekesser, Carol, ed. *Chemical Dependency: Opposing Viewpoints*. San Diego, CA: Greenhaven Press, 1997.

Organizations and Online Sites

Center for Substance Abuse Prevention
Division of Community Education
5600 Fishers Lane
Rockwall 11, Suite 800
Rockville, MD 20857
This government agency offers substance abuse prevention information.

Cocaine Anonymous World Services
http://www.ca.org/index.html

This organization provides support for people looking to end their cocaine addiction. Its online site has a directory where individuals can find meetings in their local area.

Drug War Facts
http://www.drugwarfacts.org/cocaine.htm
This online site provides basic information on cocaine and recent trends in the drug's use.

Hazelton Foundation
Pleasant Valley Road
Box 176
Center City, MN 55012-0176
This foundation provides pertinent drug information and educational materials on various aspects of drug abuse.

National Families in Action
Century Plaza II
2957 Clairmont Road
Atlanta, GA 30329
This organization offers drug prevention information and referrals for treatment.

National Institute on Drug Abuse
http://www.nida.nih.gov
The National Institute on Drug Abuse offers information on the latest drug research.

A Note on Sources

Since cocaine use is a problem with medical, social, and legal aspects, a range of sources were needed to adequately research it. Books I used which provided a good deal of information on the various facets of the drug included, *A Brief History of Cocaine* by Steven B. Karch, *Cocaine: An In-Depth Look at the Facts, Science, History and Future of the World's Most Addictive Drug* by John C. Flynn, and *Cocaine Changes: The Experience of Using and Quitting* by Dan Waldorf, Craig Reinarman, and Sheigla Murphy.

Periodicals and online sites often provide the most timely information on a subject, and the ones that best helped me gain insight into the world of cocaine were *The Journal of the American Medical Association*, *Science*, *Life*, *BioScience*, *Newsweek*, and *The New York Times*. Among the most useful online sites were "Cocaine Anonymous Ohio Online" and "Cocaine User Helping Hand."

The National Institute on Drug Abuse also provided a wealth of information for the book. Particularly helpful in providing a close-up view of the cocaine problem was its publication "Cocaine/Crack: The Big Lie." "Tips for Teens: The Truth About Cocaine" from the Center for Substance Abuse Prevention was another good source.

Many of the quotes throughout the book from those struggling with cocaine addiction are taken from the above sources. I also wish to thank those individuals who took the time to personally share their feelings with me about what life was like for them while addicted to cocaine.

—Elaine Landau

Index

Numbers in *italics* indicate illustrations.

About the
Author

Popular author Elaine Landau worked as a newspaper reporter, editor, and as a youth services librarian before becoming a full-time writer. She has written more than two hundred nonfiction books for young people. Many of her books for Franklin Watts are on health topics, including *Autism*, *Tourette Syndrome*, and *Parkinson's Disease*. Ms. Landau, who has a bachelor's degree in English and journalism from New York University and a master's degree in library and information science from Pratt Institute, lives in Florida.